# DOODLES FROM MY NOODLE

## ...a whole bunch of different poems

PAUL JENKINS

for Izzy,
PJ

First published in 2021 by Double Rainbow Publishing
www.doublerainbowpublishing.com



ISBN 978-1-9998177-6-3



Printed and bound by Book Printing UK, Remus House, Coltsfoot Drive, Woodston, Peterborough, PE2 9BF

www.pauljenkinspoet.co.uk

@teacherwriterPJ

# CONTENTS

## ABOUT THE AUTHOR

Paul Jenkins is a former teacher, turned writer, performer and radio presenter. 'Doodles From My Noodle' is Paul's 7th book of poetry following his 'Poems from Villagetown' books; 'Running with Rhythm and Rhyme' and the 'Bottom Burps' trilogy.

Since 2019 he has also worked as a radio presenter and hosts 'Waffle The Bite-Sized Podcast" where he speaks weekly to writers of poetry, comedy and anything wordy about their work.

He is also a passionate believer that telling (and listening to) each other's stories can really help to change the world.

So, he keeps on writing them.

## ABOUT THE BOOK

Well, it's poems, innit?

**For Mel,**
**as doodles only happen**
**when you feel inspired**
**to put pen to paper.**

# BEGINNING DOODLES

## Poems which sort of introduce the book a bit.

## MY SPACE

This is my space
My place
To show my face
And interlace
Some words
For you

It's a case
Of an embrace
An end
To the endless race
Where we can chase
The dreams
In this common place
Of rhyme and metre
Of wordy wonder
This onomatopoeiac buzz
For us

So please do keep apace
And have the grace
That even if
It's not your taste
We can
I hope
Find a base
To share
And trace
Through any time
And any place...

Some stories.

Trust me.

It'll be ace.

## DOODLES

I like to doodle.
Oodles of doodles.
Doodles of noodles
And doodles of poodles.
But not doodles of strudels.

Because of the spelling.

# ANIMAL DOODLES

## Poems about things that buzz, baa, flap squelch, miaow and roar.

## A BIT ODD

Yes.
She had pink hair.
Yes.
They would stop and stare.
Yes.
They'd all paid a quid.
Yes.
She was a squid.

And yes,
She was
Rather odd.

The hairy,
Neon
Cephalopod.

## PENGUINS

Penguins waddle
Penguins toddle
Penguins are
A great role model
Penguins keep
Their heads held high
Their beaks placed up
Towards the sky
They're always neat
In black tie dress
A tidy bird
They take no mess
Diet? Healthy
Loads of fish
So tonight
I think I'll wish
I was a penguin
Pootling round...

My flippers firmly on the ground

**BUSY BEE**

Buzz Buzz
Flower
Rub

Buzz Buzz
Flower Flower
Rub Rub
Rub Rub

Buzz Buzz
Flower
Buzz
Flower
Rub
Buzz Buzz
Flower
Flower
Bu-

Think.
Think.

"Did I lock the
back door?"

Think.

Buzz
Buz
Uz
Z
...

## LLAMA POLICE

Llamas have dramas
Llamas are crackers
Llamas are totally
Not alpacas

Llamas can harm ya,
But mind their own biz,
Fluffy and cuddly
Is what llamas is

As llamas love farmers
They eat the lush grass
Acting as guards
And you shall not pass!

Llamas are armour
They stop the palaver
Of midnight rustlers
In balaclavas

Llamas give karma
They've got strength and grit
They're also quite icky
As Llamas? They spit

## ADVICE ABOUT TIGERS

Do not keep a tiger in your house

You can have a little pussy cat
Or maybe have a dog
A goldfish or a snake perhaps
Perhaps you'd like a frog
A guinea pig, a hamster
A rabbit or a mouse
But please my friend

Do not keep a tiger in your house

"But they're so cute!"
I hear you say
"When they are little cubs"
"We'd wrestle on the carpet"
"And I'd give it belly rubs"
But tigers grow their paws and claws
So friends don't be a louse
My advice?

Do not keep a tiger in your house

As tigers live in jungles
Not at number twenty-three
They tend to eat quite meaty stuff
And that means you and me
They're powerful, they're beautiful
But come on, use your nous
It's simple people

Do not keep a tiger in your house!

## UN POÉME SUR UN CHAT

Je suis un chat
Mon nom est Pat
Je ne suis pas gros
Je suis assis
Sur le tapis

Miaou

## THE BRIEF TALE OF THE CHEEKY SNAIL & THE OLD MAN ASLEEP IN THE GARDEN

Old man, old man - while you sleep
Snoozing, snoring - I will creep

Gloopy travel - not a peep
While you lay there - in a heap

Climbing steady - oh so steep
Goo is oozing - it will seep

On your nose and on your cheek
When you awake - you may just weep

But I will smile and quiet I'll keep
As I watch on - from grass so deep...

Squelch.

## EUNICE

Eunice was a unicorn
Unique in every way
Not boyicorn
Not girlicorn
They only liked to play

Some of their friends had blue hair
Some friends had manes of pink
But Eunice had a rainbow
And it made all stop and think

They had the best of all worlds
And were so filled up with joy
Who cared what they were called?
They danced like every girl and boy

And so all sang together
And their song - it made them fly
Our Eunice sparkling fast and free
Across the moonlit sky

## CAT ON HEAD

Awoken from slumber
Disturbed in my bed
I appear to have
A cat on my head

Nimble and silent
Creeping so light
To share in my pillow
She crept in the night

She nestled and snuggled
And burrowed and cuddled
And now I'm awake
And I'm feeling befuddled

As she is so peaceful
It has to be said
But I am awake
With a cat on my head

# SILLY DOODLES

**Poems which no-one should really take too seriously. They're silly after all.**

## POINTLESS

This is a pointless poem
It's going nowhere fast
It's got no rhyme or reason
It isn't built to last

Oh hold on - there's a rhyme there
This verse may have direction!
Or not - it's hard to tell sometimes
I think not on reflection

I'm right - this piece is worthless
It has nothing to say
And just to contradict me...
...you read it anyway

Silly Words...

**DAS TEOP**

,sdrawkcab si etirw I gnihtyrevE

,em rof melborp gib yrev a s'tI

,pleh ylreporp t'nod srorrim nevE

(: .das em sekam tsuj hcihW

**LOUD AND PROUD**

Farts
I like 'em
I like 'em I do
I cannot escape it
They smell like poo...

They're warm and they're cosy
They're silly and fun
They rumble while exiting
Out of my bum

But no-one else likes them
They cover their nose
And tell me to leave
Which is fair I suppose

But I won't be stopping any time soon
Now I just do them alone in my room
A master of flatulence, wizard of pumps
Conductor of symphonies
Made out of trumps

**SNOW**

Snow
Whoa!
What a show.
Falls fast...
Falls slow...
It's pretty -
It's...
You know....
It's snow.

Lovely.

**BANK HOLIDAYS**

Banks get holidays
They need a little rest
They need recuperation
To do their banking best

Poets don't get holidays
We're always here on call
Writing always - 365
We don't get breaks at all

If poets took a breather
And they played that little game
This poem wouldn't be here -
And that would be a shame

**EGGS**

Soft boiled
Hard boiled
Baked or fried
Poached and scrambled
All I've tried

But nothing beats
(It has to be said)
Some toast
And my favourite…

Chocolate Egg.

**RECORD BREAKER**

A girl went down in history
She drank ten thousand cups of tea
She told them "It's the way to be -
It really is the best for me"

It seems to all a mystery
And yes, it's really clear to see
That though she's pleased
(To some degree)
She really does now need a wee...

# FEELINGS DOODLES

## Poems about happy stuff, sad stuff and all the bits in the middle.

## HEADACHE

Ow ow ow
Ow ow ow
Ow ow ow
Ow ow ow

Ow ow ow
Ow ow...
Oh?
Has it stopped?
...

No.

Ow.

## CAN'T SLEEP

*Can't sleep, Can't sleep*
*Can't sleep, Can't sleep*

What time is it?

*Can't sleep*

What day is it?

*Can't sleep*

What was that noise?

*Can't sleep*

Was it my toys?

*Can't sleep*

Are they awake?

*Can't sleep*

Such a headache!

*Can't sleep*

Why can't I sleep?

*Can't sleep*

Not even a peep!

*Can't sleep*

Sun starts to rise...

*Can't sleep*

Just close my eyes...

*Can't...*

Zzzzzz

Brrrrring!

Mum comes in....

Time for school!
Get up!
You...CAN'T SLEEP!

## GETTING OLDER

When you get old
It's a right old pain
You forget what you're doing
Again and again

You walk into rooms
Then walk straight back out
Forgetting what you...
Yeah.

Getting old
It's a right old pain
You forget what you're doing...

Hold on.

I'll be right back....

*(We apologise for the pause in the poem. The poet will return in 30 seconds or so having hopefully remembered what he came in to say.*

*He gets like this sometimes.*

*Just sit tight....*

...

*Ah. Yes. Here he is. Enjoy.)*

When you get old
It's a right old pain
You forget what you're doing
Again and again.

Turns out that was all of it.

**HOT**

29 degrees
And it is
Far too hot to rhyme
It's sticky
Icky
Humid
Oh-
It's not
A pleasant time

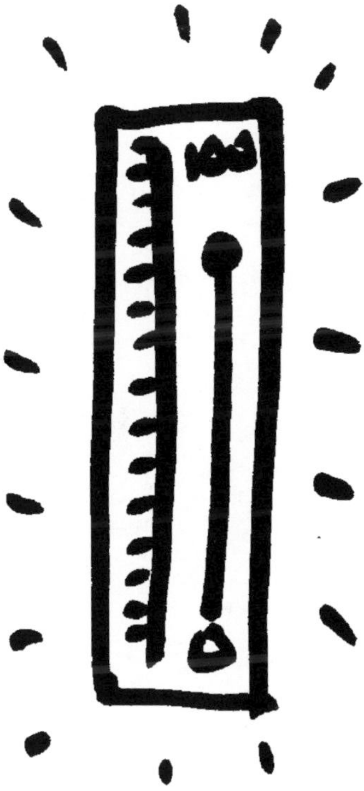


Too much
For odes or haikus
Too much
For epic rants
Just one unwelcome
Image
Of
A poet
In his pants...

## MY WORRY ABOUT OUTER SPACE

Astronauts
Are all space bound
But I'm content
Down here on ground

As if I fall
When I'm down here
It's bound to hurt
But space I fear

Is truly awful
Doubly mean
As no-one there
Can hear you scream

## MUSIC

I rave in my room
I pop in my socks
I sway to the swing
I hip-hop and rock

I groove into funk
I jive into jazz
Exploding in punk
With classic pizazz

The country is mine
In the house as I dance
In a square, in a line
I'm hardcore, I'm trance

With breakbeats and backbeats
Reggae and blues
K-Pop to B-Bop
And ambient snooze

Reggae and gospel
Dubstep and grunge
I'm like the world's jukebox
A musical sponge

So turn up the radio
Dial to eleven
As when I hear music
I'm truly in heaven.

## BRAINS

How do you get
A noggin that works?
And not one that
Buzzes and swizzles
And twerks?

And makes
All the bungles
And duff ups
And mess?

And leaves you
With stresses
And stresses
And stress....

Is it just me?

It's not?

Oh that's good.

Cos I've got explosions
Hid under this hood

At least I know now
That you all get them too
And my brain's not broken

I guess that'll do.

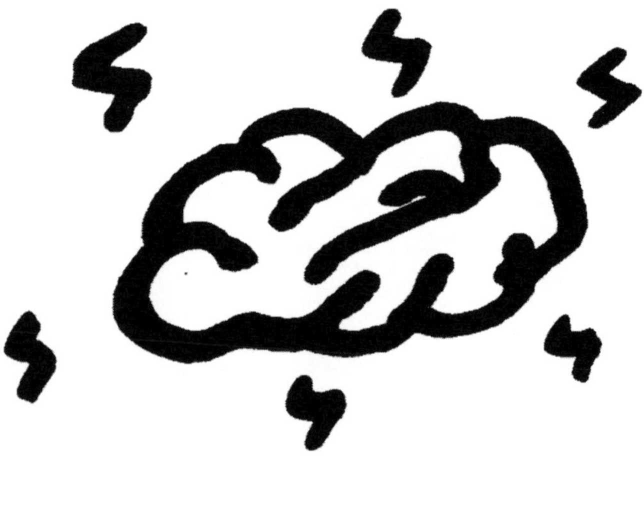

## FIGHT HATE WITH DISCO

Fight hate with Disco
Get them where it grooves
Every time a name is called
Bust out awesome moves

Each tweet that's venomous
Each post untrue
Shine a light with glitterballs
Is what you have to do

Turn their fight to funky
End the daily blues
Celebrate good times - come on!
Then we will never lose

Make them dance and make them sing
And make them feel the joy
Till every tiny bit of nasty
Leaves each girl and boy

And if they do not listen?
Then it's time to party loud
As everybody knows that hate
Sounds rubbish in a crowd

Fill that floor with sparkle
Make the evil cease
Boogie till the haters
Learn to live with all in peace

## HOPE

What is hope?
Well...
It's hard to say.

I hope my team
Are the best at play...
That I won't get lost
When I go this way...
Or this lovely weather
Is here to stay...

I hope I'll know
Which words to say...
My bus arrives
With no delay...
And I hope you're with me
Come what may-

Forever
Every single day.

So, what is hope?

A wish and a dream
That in the future
Things will seem

Brighter, lighter,
Filled with style,
And bursting with
A billion smiles.

# SPORTY DOODLES

## Poems about running around, whizzing around and getting all sweaty around.

## CUDDLY BOXER

Boxing is so difficult
I get bomped on the nose
One hit and I just wobble
Then I'm knocked right off my toes

I'm not that great with bruises
And my teeth seem better straight
It all feels quite a trauma
Being beaten up's not great

But I like the way we cuddle
In the middle of the ring
I'll win the gold I'm certain
Hugs are totally my thing

## SK8ER GRRL

I wish I'd learned
To ride the rails
When I was just thirteen
To flip 360s
Jumps and tricks
Be goofy on the scene

I would have soared
And floated free
I'd ollie, flip and fake
Extending every
Twist and turn
Some golden air I'd take

Oh to be
Thirteen again
Just boards and hips and hills
Not a care
Or worry dude
Live life just for the thrills

## BLADETASTIC

They call us the flyers
The speed renegades
Strength & precision
Momentum on blades

The spring in our step
Gives us push, power, flow
And once we get moving
Oh wow, can we go!

All down the straight
Right round the bends
Sometimes for hours
Our race never ends

Training to be
The best of the best
To leave them for dust
To beat all the rest

To cross the line first
Like our heroes of old
To sprint Paralympic
And bring home the gold!

## GOLDEN COUPLE

(A poem for Team Kenny*)

There once was a girl
And there once was a boy
Who played out on bikes
And it filled them with joy

They pedalled and pedalled
And pedalled some more
They laughed and they joked
Like they hadn't before

A spark then appeared
On their wheels as they rode
Riding with love in their veins
And it showed

Not only a passion
To train and to race
But a fire in their eyes
And a smile on their face

One for each other
Not tandem but team
To help one another
They lived all our dreams

Of a fantasy tale
Like the stories we're told
Of love and of triumph
Our couple of gold

**Laura & Jason Kenny are British cyclists. They are married and between them have won lots and lots of cycling medals – making them the most successful married couple in Summer Olympic history.*

## NONE HUNDRED AND GIGGLES (THEN NOT GIGGLES)

Tony threw a dart
It missed the board by miles
It went right out the window
And caused a fair few smiles

As Tony claimed that evening
Before he took the oche
That he was once World Champion
He'd been a little cocky

Now everyone was laughing
As they knew he'd told a lie
A giant one, a whopper
A humungous porky pie

But someone wasn't laughing
As the dart fell to the ground
A string without a red balloon
And crying all around...

# LAST MINUTE PENALTY

There's the ball
On the spot
There's the keeper
There's the shot

There's the glove
There's the dive
There's the save - they survive!

There's the party
There's the crowd
There's the army
Shouting loud
Like they've gone and won the cup
Singing "We are staying up!!!"

No such fun for my team though
No elation
No big show
As though we're great
(And more than able)
My lot always float mid table

# PEOPLE DOODLES

## Poems about family, friends and made-up people who never really existed at all.

## FRENEMY

We’re frenemies
The best of foes
We smile and squash
Each other’s toes

Two siblings
Born two years apart
We’ve turned our squabbles
Into art

A clash of kin
The hair-pull twisters
Bosom baddies
Nemesisters

Bickering from noon till night
Snapping
Slapping
Fight and fight

But upset one
You'll soon see two
Towering
Glowering
Over you

Discovering
How thick blood is
And how our sting
Is like our hiss

Lethal
If we come together
Turning tides
And changing weather

Moving mountains
Causing quakes
Cross my sister?
Big mistake

There's only one
Can cause her grief
The one who's
Just the same beneath

Love her
Hate her
You will see
You'll not dare touch
My frenemy

## THE GREATEST FAMILY BAND

We've got the greatest family band
It's really something rather grand
Writing hits, creating sounds
Music that is quite profound

Cutting edge is what we bring
We don't just sit on stools and sing
Oh no, we've got more talent dude
A dynasty with attitude

I'm the frontman - singing star
Dad's on bass - and Mum guitar
Cousin Jim and Cousin John
Noodle banjos all night long

Uncle Terry toots the toot
On saxophone and sometimes flute
Auntie Mabel on viola
Techno, hip-hop, bossa nova

Betty-Jane (who's only five)
Plays Kazoo and does the jive
Grandma DJ's bangin' choons
While Grandad sits
And plays the spoons

Then the dogs and cats join in
We really make an awful din
But luckily we style it out
We make the crowds
All scream and shout

In fact the noise can sometimes be
Too much for Pat at number three
It's not long till we know the score
With PC 'Shush now' at the door

**MUMS**

They fill up your tums.
They pick up your crumbs.
They help with your sums.
And give you wine gums.
They've all got bums.

Mums.

## GRUBBY GIRL

I'm the grubby girl
Who lives on your street
Crumpled shirt
And never neat

A mountain of earth
Kept under my nails
From digging and playing
With slugs and with snails

If I was allowed to
I'd live in the dirt
With muck and with mud
Caked all over my skirt

Climbing up trees
And scuffing my shoes
A life spent exploring
The one that I'd choose

A big cheesy grin
As I splash through the streams
Look at my face
It just beams and it beams

Dust on my shoes
And twigs in my hair
You think I look dirty?
I don't really care

I'm the grubby girl
Who lives up your way
The scruffiest Princess
Of outdoor play

## BIBBLY BOB

Bibbly Bob was a bubbly boo
Bibbing and bobbing
Like all bubbles do
He walloped and dolloped
And bounced all around
With billowing bellows
And bumbling sounds

But one day he bobbled
And bubbled too high
A bobbing balloon
Blowing into the sky

So bobbles beware
When your bibbles go bop
You may find your bobbling
Comes to a stop

And boom!
All your bobbles
Will fall on the floor
And like our poor Bob
You will bubble no more

## CAVE DUDE

Me is cave dude
Me stone carve
Me survivor
Me not starve

Me is cave dude
Me make thing
Thing that help move
Thing that spin

Me is cave dude
Me catch beast
Me drag back home
Me bring feast

Me is cave dude
Me make hot
Me make food nice
Me like lot

Me is cave dude
Me impressed
You make bronze now
Me get stressed

Me like Stone Age
But me think
Cave dudes like me
All extinct

## TUESDAY NIGHTS

Tuesday night
Is pasta night
Is cola night
Dessert night

It's film night
And game night
It's bowling night
And late night

It's picking up at four night
It's dropping off at school night
It's got to keep on time night
It's keeping things all sweet night

Remembering your bag night
Remembering your shoes night
Remembering your tie night
"Is your uniform all here?" night

It's different than it was night
It is just what it is night
It's spend some time with Dad night
Perfect? Well it's not quite

But it is still a good night
We try to all get on night
As it is just for one night
And that is how we stay tight

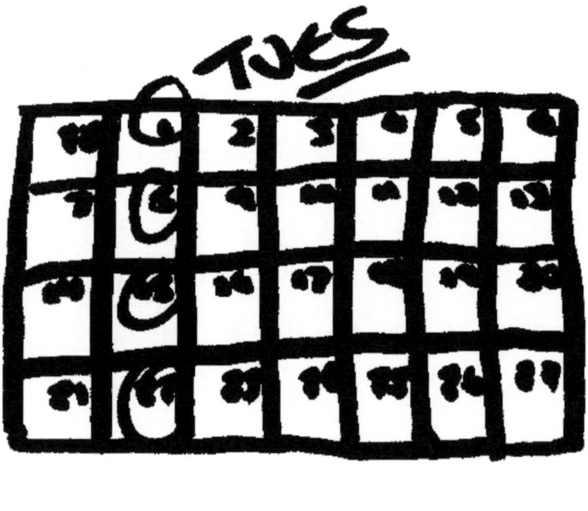

# THINGS DOODLES

Poems about things. You know, those things that are all over the place. Stuff.

## SOCK WOE

When one loses a sock
It isn't nice to mock
As one without a pair
Isn't quite so debonair...

## MY BED

Lovely
Comfy
Flumphy
Squmphy
Big and soft
And plush
And plumphy

It's so nice
I'll stay right here
Tucked up tight
In bed all year

**MUGS**

I think we've got
A thousand mugs
Too many for our shelf
Stacked ones
Cracked ones
They all arrived by stealth

A birthday here
A Christmas there
A joke for Father's Day
Big ones
Small ones
We're like a small cafe

Yet all of them
Have memories
So through them I will sift
Loved ones
Shared ones
Each one a perfect gift

## BONG

Big Ben
Bing bongs

A big bad
Booming bell

Every hour
Every day

For centuries as well

But sometimes
Big Ben's bell don't bong
As things need to be mended
And people end up
Turning up
Much later than intended

## MY ROCK

I carried this rock from Damascus
Where my father once worked in a bank
We left as the bullets came closer
The day that we saw the first tank

I carried it over the mountains
I held it at night in our tent
I carried it over the water
But only I knew what it meant

And now my rock sits on my table
While I work at school all the while
Forever beside me, my dad watches on
I'm safe now and that makes him smile

# ONE LAST DOODLE

**The end of the book. Something to put a bit of a spring in your step.**

**A LAST WORD**

You're best at doing
What you do
And what you do?
It's up to you

Don't hold back
For those who sigh
"The risk of failure
Is too high"

Try not to listen
To that voice
The one that limits
Daily choice

The one that nags you
"Don't be brave...
Don't chase dreams...
The things you crave...

Hide away...
Don't show your face...
Keep quiet...
In your safest place..."

That voice
That ever-tightening tie
That binds us down
And bleeds us dry

Break free! Take life
On boldest terms
Say it daily
Reaffirm

You know best
Who you should be
Not them
And not society

No time to stop
Or to conform
No time for being
Uniform

A force
That cannot be subdued
Sparkling
Gleaming
Dazzling
You